s h a m a n i s m

shamanism

RITUALS FOR SPIRIT JOURNEYING AND SACRED SPACE

william adcock

southwater

This edition is published by Southwater

Distributed in the UK by
The Manning Partnership
251–253 London Road East
Batheaston
Bath BA1 7RL
UK
tel. (0044) 01225 852 727
fax (0044) 01225 852 852

Distributed in Australia by
Sandstone Publishing
Unit 1, 360 Norton Street
Leichhardt
New South Wales 2040
Australia
tel. (0061) 2 9560 7888
fax (0061) 2 9560 7488

Distributed in New Zealand
by
Five Mile Press NZ
PO Box 33-1071
Takapuna
Auckland 9
New Zealand
tel. (0064) 9 4444 144

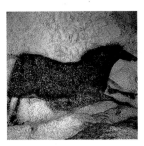

Southwater is an imprint of Anness Publishing Limited
© 2000 Anness Publishing Limited
1 3 5 7 9 10 8 6 4 2

Publisher: Joanna Lorenz
Senior Editor: Joanne Rippin
Additional prose: Will Adcock
Photographer: Don Last
Stylist: Lucy Pettifer
Designer: Ruth Hope
Production Controller:
Yolande Denny

CONTENTS

INTRODUCTION

The old man's breath came in white puffs as he chanted softly, almost inaudibly, in his slowly spinning progression around the wheel, circles within a circle. He had been dancing and chanting for hours and now, as he sensed the climax of the ritual, his spinning became more animated, whirling him around the circle he had created with his stamping feet. In a triumphant finale he scooped a double armful of snow from the eastern gateway and hurled it skywards, watching the uppermost ice crystals catch the light of the returning sun. Arms raised aloft, the shaman greeted the beginning of the sunrise that heralded the end of the long winter night.

Shamanism is essentially a state of mind, a way of viewing life as a whole. The shaman gains insights and wisdom by connecting with other parts of creation and healing the divisions that exist between the separate pieces. Such divisions can occur anywhere: within the self, within groups, between people and the environment, and so on.

The word shaman comes from the Tungusic dialect of the Ural-Altaic tribes of Siberia. Shamans were the priest-doctors of the tribes, responsible for officiating at ceremonies and rituals, tending the sick and caring for all aspects of the spiritual wellbeing of the people.

Shamanism does not recognize age, gender, race or religious doctrines and so is available to all. Indeed, many people have shamanic experiences without labelling them as such. It could even be said that some important scientific discoveries have been instigated by shamanic experiences. Humans are a part of creation and shamanism is our way of connecting with the whole. It is a fundamental part of our heritage and, although the connection may be weakened by modern life, the ability to connect, and the inclination to do so, is still present. This book is an introduction to shamanic practices, it will guide you towards wisdom through rituals, journeying, and working with dreams.

A SHAMAN'S JOURNEY BEGINS WITH THE BEAT OF THE DRUM.

THE TRADITION OF THE SHAMAN

A KAMCHATKA SHAMAN DANCING WITH A DRUM.

When communities were much more isolated and self-reliant than modern society is, shamans played an integral part in their cultures, performing numerous and specific duties. They practised healing in cases of sickness and injury, but they were not specifically healers. Although they communed with ancestors, spirits and gods, they were not exclusively priests, and while they offered wise counsel to their communities, they were not solely sages. Rather, they fulfilled a combination of these roles and others besides.

THE SHAMAN'S ROLE

To understand the function of a shaman, it is necessary to adopt a world view relative to traditional peoples. Typically, older cultures more in touch with the natural world have been animistic societies. Animism is a term derived from the Latin *anima*, which means soul, and these older cultures held the belief that all things possessed a soul or spirit. The fundamental role of the shaman was to act as an intermediary in relating to the other spirits of the earth: the animals, the land, the rain, the crops and so on. Because humans were so dependent on the forces of nature and the other beings of the planet,

communicating with them was seen as a way of predicting problems or finding a way out of them. The shaman could send his or her soul out on a journey to meet with these other spirits and ensure a successful hunt or determine why a crop was failing, or if there would be a drought. These journeys of the soul could also lead shamans to other dimensions where they would commune with gods,

A NORTH AMERICAN BLACKFOOT SHAMAN IN CEREMONIAL ROBES.

find special knowledge or acquire powers which gave them an advantage when living in difficult times or healing the sick.

It was this ability to travel at will to other realms that marked out the shaman. Very often it was unlooked for, with visions occurring spontaneously, or caused by traumatic experiences such as severe illness or injury. What is often termed "madness" in modern western society was seen as being "touched by the gods" by traditional people. Shamans usually lived somewhat apart from the rest of the community, because their powers made them different from other people. However, individuals who were able to hear voices and experience realities beyond the normal scope of perception were regarded with respect and awe.

SHAMANIC JOURNEYING

These altered states of consciousness could also be induced by a shaman seeking to go on a journey. The drum was a very powerful shamanic tool, seen as a mode of transporting the soul on its regular beat as it opened gateways for the shaman. Dancing was another method employed to achieve a trance state, usually to contact a specific animal spirit. By moving the body in a way that mimicked the animal in question, the shaman became that animal and was able to relate directly to it. Costume was also important in this respect and the use of feathers, skins, bones and significant designs was seen as a way of linking with spirits and journeying to other dimensions.

Sacred plants have a long history of being used as a means of accessing the spirit worlds. In Europe, fly agaric, psilocybe mushrooms and doses of hemlock were all used

as vehicles by which a shaman could enter an altered state of consciousness. In Mexico, the peyote cactus was, and still is, eaten in a ritual that takes many hours. The trance state it induces brings the shaman into contact with the spirit of the universe, who grants visions and gives knowledge. In South America the principal sacred plant is the banisteriopsis vine, which has also been used for a long time. The

ANIMAL SKINS HELPED A SHAMAN COMMUNE WITH THE SPIRITS.

plant is brewed into a drink known as *ayahuasca* or *yagé*, which is drunk in a ceremony. It produces similar effects to those of peyote, inducing visionary trances and heightened telepathic abilities which allow the shaman to "tune in" to the different levels of creation or travel to otherworlds.

Because of the powers of these sacred plants, they need to be approached with respect. Their gathering and preparation involves a lengthy ritual incorporating prayers and offerings to the spirits of the plants that can take many hours or even days.

Shamans, then, held a position of influence but also one of great responsibility. The people would turn to them first in matters of importance, and the shamans would use their abilities and powers to find a satisfactory outcome.

LEGENDARY SHAMANS

In the European cultures there are many myths of shamans and shamanic adventures. Ceridwen was a great Celtic shaman who brewed a magic potion to confer infinite knowledge on her son. However, it was inadvertently tasted by her kitchen boy, who thus acquired all her wisdom. During a shapeshifting chase to catch him, she became a hen and he a grain of corn.

THE YOUNG ARTHUR RECEIVES TEACHING FROM MERLIN.

Ceridwen ate the corn and became pregnant with the Celtic bard, Taliesin.

In the Arthurian legends, Merlin possessed divinatory powers and could shapeshift, commune with animals and spirits and travel to the otherworlds.

MERLIN DICTATES HIS HISTORY.

Odin, the chief god of the Aesir in the Scandinavian Pantheon, was another famous shaman. He gave up one of his eyes in return for a drink from the well of Mimir, the water of which was the source of all wisdom. He also sacrificed himself on the World Tree to learn the wisdom of the dead, bringing back runes from the underworld.

MODERN SHAMANISM

Traditional shamanism still exists in many places in the world, especially where the old cultures remain strong. It is not uncommon for people to seek the assistance of a shaman in the lands of the Arctic, Africa, Australasia, Indonesia, North and South America, Mongolia, China and Tibet. Although in modern western societies there seems to be little need for a shaman to help with problems about food, the weather or disgruntled gods, there is a place for shamanism on a personal level. Shamanism is a way to find our place in the universe. By embarking upon a shamanic journey to other levels of consciousness, the modern shaman can reach depths of insight that can lead to personal growth and enlightenment.

ONE-EYED ODIN ON HIS MAGICAL STEED, SLEIPNIR.

Connecting with Spirit

What is spirit? How can it be defined? Spirit is the omnipresent energy possessed by all things. It is the essence of creation, the unifying force that is present throughout the universe. Spirit connects us one with another, but also with animals, plants, rocks, water, air, the stars and the space between the stars. It is the skein of being beyond the physical that can be accessed for communication, for healing and for understanding.

Imagine a spider's web, a beautifully delicate construction designed to catch flies and transmit vibrations. The structure is continuous, so that the whole is affected to some degree wherever an insect is trapped in it. Moreover, the spider can differentiate between the struggling of a trapped fly and the vibration set up by, say, the wind or an airborne seed. The simile of a web is used in many traditional societies to illustrate the principle of connectedness, and the same analogy is used in the modern world – in the World Wide Web, the information superhighway, which permits worldwide communication in virtually no time at all. Just think of the energy incorporated here – energy that is an extension of the universal energy, the spirit of creation.

Of course, the universal connection is more complex than the tracery created by a single spider, or even the myriad connections of the internet, because there are webs within webs. The spirit web of the human race is made up of smaller webs of friends and family; the spiritual web of life on Earth is an amalgamation of humans, animals, plants, rocks and water.

ENERGY IS APPARENT ALL AROUND US.

The fundamental link in the web is energy. Energy suffuses all things, but the energy of each part of creation vibrates at its own particular frequency. The energy encompassed by an entity, be it a rock, a blade of grass or a human being, is an extension of the web of spirit, and the extent to which you can affect and be affected by communication on the network depends upon how receptive you are.

All of us are aware of energy on an instinctive level. We have all experienced atmospheres; in a room after an argument has occurred so much energy has been emitted that the air is thick with it. On a more subtle level, there is the instinctive feeling that you are liked or disliked by someone. Because humans have closely linked vibrations, the energy is readily sensed by other humans. A shaman can extend this sensitivity to feel the vibrations of other parts of creation.

A SPIDER'S WEB ILLUSTRATES CONNECTEDNESS.

THE NIGHT SKY IS A POTENT REMINDER OF THE UNIVERSALITY OF CREATION.

SACRED SPACE

There are many examples of sacred sites around the world that have special significance to particular societies: Stonehenge for the Druids; Mount Olympus for the Greeks; the San Francisco Mountains for the native American Zuni tribe; the Black Hills of South Dakota for the plains tribes; and Uluru (formerly known as Ayers Rock) for the Australian tribes. These sites are usually powerful places associated with the ancestors, gods or spirits of a given culture. They are important to the collective psyche of the society. Sacred space approaches the concept on a more personal level.

Is there a place that you find especially conducive to meditation or relaxation? Perhaps a tree in a park or your garden, a certain rock outcrop or a wood where you often walk. Anywhere that you feel comfortable can be a sacred space, and that includes a place within yourself; sometimes it's not possible to travel physically to a special place to unwind just when you need to, so why not carry it with you?

YOUR SACRED SPACE IS A SAFE, SECURE PLACE.

The inner sacred space is a place that you create as a sanctuary, a retreat from the physical world, where you can relax and recoup your energy, so it can resemble anything that makes you feel comfortable: a desert island, a hut on a mountain, a cave, anything. Maybe it's a place that you already know; somewhere you have visited in a dream or in this world. The more you visualize, the more real it will seem, so try to feel textures, see details, hear sounds and smell scents.

Your sacred space is a safe place and, because it is always there, you can visit it at any time. It can evolve as much as you want it to, because you created it and the control over it lies only with you. The only limitations are ones that you, as the maker, impose. So, be aware of what comes into being, for that can offer important insights into your subconscious. This private place is a good jumping-off point for beginning journeys.

STONEHENGE IN WILTSHIRE, ENGLAND, IS AN ANCIENT SACRED SITE FOR THE DRUIDS.

EXPERIENCING NATURE

The natural world is a great place to find peace, tranquillity and inspiration, and to practise visualizing details to put into your own sacred space. Get out as much as possible to experience the benefits that a natural environment can bring. When out walking, be aware of your surroundings, admire the beauty of a tree or a bird in flight and always be grateful. Life is a precious gift to be appreciated now.

Nature can give us many things to help remind us of our connection – stones, feathers, sticks, intricate patterns and images – but if anything is taken, remember to leave something in return as an offering, an exchange of energy to signify your appreciation of the gift that has been given to you. Shamanism is about relating to the natural world and our place in it. Take time to stop, relax and meditate on the incredible complexity of the creation around you. Close your eyes and see how much sharper your other senses become. Extend that receptivity to feel the land, and blend with it. Feel what is around you: the vitality of the earth, the immensity of the world and the universe beyond. You are a part of it, be aware and accept the experience for what it is: humbling and precious.

PRACTISING SHAMANISM IN A NATURAL SETTING ENHANCES THE BOND BETWEEN YOU AND THE WORLD AROUND YOU.

REGULAR VISITS TO THE COUNTRYSIDE HELP TO CONNECT YOU WITH OTHER PARTS OF CREATION.

VISUALIZING SACRED SPACE

Before you begin journeying or dreamwork you need to work on visualizing a place in your mind that becomes your own personal sacred space. The sacred space you create will be your place and only people you invite may enter. It can be any kind of place in which your spirit feels happy and at home: a woodland clearing, a cave, a deserted beach, even a corner of your own garden. The more times you visit your sacred space the more real it will seem and the easier it will be to get there. Concentrate on creating and remembering detail; love the place, care for it, plant flowers and trees and tend them as they grow, decorate it as you would your home. Work out rituals for arriving and leaving and, from time to time, imagine making an offering there to help express your gratitude.

ENTERING YOUR SACRED SPACE

Use these steps to build and enter your sacred space. As with all shamanic practices it is good to begin with a calm state of mind. Breathe from your diaphragm and release any worries. When you feel relaxed, picture your spirit body stepping out of your physical body. Your spirit body is beautiful, glowing, solid and real, connected to your earthly body by a thin filament. Look down at yourself, sitting or lying peacefully, before you start the journey.

1 Take five deep breaths to centre yourself and focus your mind on what you are about to do. Voice your intent out loud. Light a candle and burn some incense, holding your intention in your mind.

2 Contemplate the candle flame for a while, imagining it lighting up the recesses inside you so that you may find a way to the place you seek more easily.

3 When you feel ready to start, sit or lie down comfortably, somewhere you won't be disturbed, and focus on your breathing. With closed eyes, take deep, slow breaths from your diaphragm to keep relaxed.

USE ALL YOUR SENSES TO MAKE THE PLACE AS REAL AS POSSIBLE.

EXPANDING THE VISUALIZATION

Now picture an opening: a natural doorway such as a hole in the ground or the mouth of a cave. This will lead you to the sacred space you seek. When you pass through, pay attention to details that will make the place seem

THE ENTRANCE TO YOUR PERSONAL SPACE COULD BE A CAVE.

more real. Utilize all your senses to give the place solidity. This is tricky, but with a bit of practice it will get easier.

Expand your senses. Touch trees and feel the texture of the bark; sit on a rock and feel its surface – is it smooth or rough? Feel the warmth of the sun as you walk through the place. What is beneath your feet? Grass, sand, a path? Pause to smell the delicate fragrance of a flower, the

bloom redolent with its essence of attraction. Look into it and notice how bright the colours are and how the petals and stamens are arranged. Hear the birdsong and the sighing of the wind. Sit by a stream, taste the refreshing coolness of the water and absorb the beauty and peace.

When you feel it is time to leave, give thanks and promise to return. Retrace your steps through the entrance, back your physical body. Come slowly back to this world.

PICTURE THE SMALLEST AND MOST INTRICATE DETAIL.

ALTARS

We're all familiar with altars, and the term probably conjures up some richly decorated object that may be seen in a temple or a church, but of course they don't have to be like that. Altars serve primarily to focus the attention, so big, brightly coloured ones are good for large places. A small personal altar, using something like a stone or a log, can be placed in your home or garden and will serve the same purpose for you. It needn't be showy, although bright colours have a greater impact on the subconscious, and therefore a greater power.

Altars can be adorned with anything that has a special significance to the user, such as crystals, feathers, flowers or sticks. An altar is also a place to leave offerings. The rituals of decorating and making offerings help to reinforce your connection with the universe; the intent is paramount and the conscious reiteration reminds the physical self of the bond.

NATURAL ALTARS

You may come across a special place when out walking, such as a tree or a rock, which you can use as a temporary altar on which to celebrate that particular moment in time. Being in a more public place, it also has the advantage that others might see it and add their energy to the place.

ALTARS OUTSIDE CAN ALSO BE SEEN BY OTHERS.

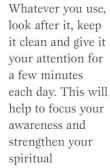

INDOOR ALTARS

An altar can be made using a flat rock or a piece of wood or a small table. Whatever you use, look after it, keep it clean and give it your attention for a few minutes each day. This will help to focus your awareness and strengthen your spiritual connections.

A SIMPLE INDOOR ALTAR.

NATURAL ALTARS CAN SHOW APPRECIATION FOR THE MOMENT.

Trees make very beautiful natural altars, pleasing to the eye and very calming when attention is focused upon them. Being firmly rooted, a tree has a deep connection with Mother Earth and that energy can be tapped into when you talk to it, leave offerings and pray or meditate there. You can tie things in the branches for decoration, or place tiny items in the trunk. A flat rock placed at the base of the trunk can serve as an altarstone. Be aware of which trees attract you, because they all have their own attributes and symbolism. For example, oak is the keeper of wisdom and possesses great strength; willow represents love and regeneration: being able to grow a new tree from a cut branch; the very tall and graceful beech symbolizes aspirations to higher ideals; yew, associated with ancient burial sites, represents transformation and inner wisdom.

Rocks are the bones of the Mother, supporting her and therefore us. Because they take millions of years to form, they hold ancient Earth wisdom and knowledge, power and strength. They aid in connecting with the Earth because they are so much a part of it, being formed deep within. Call upon this strength when you pray at a rock altar and feel it helping you, supporting you and connecting you.

MAKING A CAIRN

The beauty of making something to use as an altar is that the maker's energy is blended with the materials in a focused way. A cairn looks like a haphazard pile of stones but, to make it stable, care must be taken in selecting stones that fit together well. Take your time as you gather the stones and lay them.

1 Begin by selecting a few large, flat, roughly circular rocks to act as the base of the cairn.

2 Start to build up a tapering dome by laying smaller flat rocks in an overlapping pattern.

3 As you work, keep the intent of honouring creation, and that will help focus your energy.

4 When the cairn is complete, decorate it with objects found close by.

STONE CIRCLES

There are many examples of these ancient structures, especially in the British Isles and other parts of Northern Europe. The full purposes for their construction are unclear, although they are accurate astronomical calendars in which certain stones align with celestial bodies at significant times of the year, such as the summer and winter solstices. In North America there are large circles outlined in stone, at a number of sites. These wheels are orientated to the compass and constructed on sacred sites where people still come to pray and leave offerings.

THE INTENT BEHIND ANCIENT STONE CIRCLES IS OBSCURE BUT THEY HAVE A SIMPLE, AWE-INSPIRING MAJESTY SUCH AS THIS ONE AT CASTLERIGG, CUMBRIA, ENGLAND.

MAKING A STONE CIRCLE

Create a sacred space to honour the circle of life and your place in it with your own stone circle. Select seven stones, one each for the four directions, one for Mother Earth, one for the spirit and one for the self.

1 Bless and place the direction stones first, beginning with the east. Each of the directions has its own symbolism and energy.

2 Bless each stone before you lay it in place. Put the three remaining stones inside the circle formed by the four direction stones.

3 The completed stone circle can be used as an altar: as a place to pray, and to give thanks and gain insights into the progression of your life-path.

BLESSING THE STONES

The **east** is the place of illumination, the place of conception. It is the direction represented by spring with all its vigorous new growth. Call on this energy as you bless the stone and place it in the east position.

The **south** is the place of consolidation, the place of the child. It is the direction represented by summer when the burgeoning life progresses into fullness. Call on this energy as you bless the stone and place it in the south position.

The **west** is the place of fruition, the place of the adult. It is associated with autumn when the growth reaches its ripeness. Call on this energy as you bless the stone and place it in the west position.

The **north** is the place of calm reflection, the place of the elder. It is represented by winter, the season when the strength is drawn in. When the growth cycle is past, the elder has the wisdom of experience to reflect upon. Call upon this energy as you bless the stone and place it in the north position.

The stone for **Mother Earth** is to honour her and thank her for the gifts she gives, the food and shelter she provides, the air she breathes into us and the water that supports us. Recognize her and give thanks as you bless the stone and place it in the circle at the 11 o'clock position, near the centre.

The stone for the **spirit** is to honour and give thanks for all of creation of which we humans are a part. Recognize the bond as you bless the stone and place it in the circle at the one o'clock position, near the centre.

The stone for the **self** is to acknowledge the individual's part in the whole and to give thanks for all the things that come to you. Honour the connection as you bless the stone and place it in the circle at the six o'clock position, near the centre.

SYMBOLS

Firelight flickered across the walls of the cave as the shaman sought for a place where the symbol belonged. The dancing shadows played over the frieze of figures already depicted; simple delineations that nevertheless showed the beasts in awesome depth. Aurochs stood four-square with the majestic sweep of their horns held high, horses galloped in a swirl of graceful lines, eagles swooped on widespread wings. And somewhere amongst all these forms was a site for the symbol from last night's dream. Somewhere... There! Taking brush in hand, the shaman approached and began to paint.

Rock art – paintings in caves and under overhangs, etchings on cliffs and boulders – can be found all over the world, from Europe to Africa, America to China. The pictures span a great length of time, the oldest so far discovered being dated at about 35,000 years old. They are all symbols that inspired the cultures that they relate to.

Before writing was developed, important information was passed on orally, but our ancestors also used symbolic representations to reinforce aspects of their lives. In this way, pictures of hunting scenes acted as positive visualizations for the successful outcome of a hunt, or as a record of an event, as well as honouring the animals and their importance. Pictures of crops were positive visualizations of good harvests as well as a recognition of the gifts of the Earth. Certain symbols, such as masks or totems, were boundary markers for a

RIGHT: CAVE PAINTING OF AN AUROCHS, SPAIN.

LEFT: HUMAN FIGURES.

GALLOPING HORSE, LASCAUX CAVE PAINTING.

club insignia, each one a symbol that conveys a wealth of meaning simply and succinctly.

People have used symbols for millennia, as charms for luck, protection, health and inspiration. A symbol has its own energetic vibration and this is what influences the spirit. In the rock art of the ancestors, there are certain symbols that appear in many ancient places around the world, and from many different periods, indicating their fundamental universal importance for the human spirit. Among these powerful signs, or sigils, are the spiral and the circle in their various forms.

particular group of people. Other rock art scenes show human figures with animal characteristics such as antlers and wings: these are representative of shapeshifting in shamanic journeys, where a shaman will adopt another form for learning, healing or communication. Some cave art shows the ritual acting out of day-to-day activities such as hunting, with human figures that could be shamanic taking part. Such paintings indicate the antiquity of shamanism.

Even today, a modern version of rock art can be seen in urban settings. The graffiti seen on so many concrete cliffs are symbols that have significance, to their makers at least. Modern symbolism doesn't stop there, though. Think of all the various symbols that surround us: from national flags to advertising logos, religious icons to currency signs, and

A LASCAUX CAVE PAINTING OF A HUMAN FIGURE, POSSIBLY A SHAMAN, TAKING PART IN A HUNTING RITUAL.

SPIRALS AND CIRCLES

The spiral is an evocative image, symbolic of a life path, the lessons and learning that come to an individual through their life. A spiral is formed by tracing a point that is moving simultaneously out and around. The circular motion relates to the cyclic nature of existence, and the outward motion to the spiritual and emotional growth of a person as they progress through life, apparently repeating experiences, but each time moving to a new level.

Sometimes, spirals are combined to make double or even triple forms. Double spirals symbolize the duality of life and the natural world, seen in abundant pairs of complementary opposites, such as light and dark, young and old, mind and body – the spiritual and physical.

In Celtic lore, the triple spiral relates to the three stages of life: maiden, mother and crone. This symbol displays the cycles that are present within cycles, showing that the whole is made up of different periods of growth and development but that each stage is directly linked to the others. The spiral is also representative of a pathway, usually downwards and inwards, that a shaman may take to reach another realm.

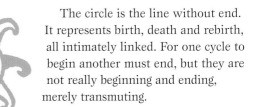

Another spiral form, especially prevalent in the Celtic tradition and still seen even today, is the spiral maze, which has the same symbolism as the more ordinary design, that of learning wisdom through initiation and experience.

THE CELTIC TRIPLE SPIRAL RELATED TO THE THREE STAGES OF LIFE: MAIDEN, MOTHER AND CRONE.

The circle is the line without end. It represents birth, death and rebirth, all intimately linked. For one cycle to begin another must end, but they are not really beginning and ending, merely transmuting.

The circle symbolizes the cycles which are present in all of creation, the relentless progress of life in all its forms. Many traditional dwellings reflected this and were of circular construction, symbolizing living within the whole. Circles that incorporate another solid circle inside, speak of the totality of creation, showing that all things are connected and that creation encompasses the individual.

SUNBURST DESIGN SHOWING AN ARROW-HEADED SPIRIT LINE.

A MEDICINE WHEEL SIMPLY MARKED OUT IN STONES.

The sunburst with a spirit line inside it is another circular symbol, evoking the image of the creative essence of the universe breathing life into all things.

MEDICINE WHEEL

Also known as the sacred hoop, the medicine wheel is used to help meditation and is a symbol of Native American spiritual beliefs. It is a circle bisected by two lines, which symbolize the blue road of spirit (east to west) and the red road of life (south to north). The resulting four sections of the circle represent the seasons of the year. As with the stone circle, each cardinal point is associated with a direction of the compass, and with particular attributes that can be related to times and situations in your own life. The east is the place of inspiration and the inception of a new idea. Progressing around the wheel, the next direction is south, related to consolidation of the cycle. West is the place where the fruits of an endeavour can be harvested. The final direction is north, the place to recuperate and reflect.

The circle can be used to relate to your position in a given cycle, and to find the best course of action to take to see a natural outcome: to decide whether you should be starting something new, or to concentrate on nurturing what you have at present, accepting the gains from a situation or drawing your strength in.

USING HERBS AND INCENSE

AN ANCIENT JEWISH PRIEST USING INCENSE.

When performing shamanic practices it is good to begin by preparing yourself spiritually and physically, to approach the undertaking in an open and honest manner. Purifying is a very positive act, which simultaneously cleanses the spirit and relaxes the body.

Incense has long been used in many cultures as a means of spiritual cleansing. The scent acts at a physical level, inducing a sense of calm and relaxation, while the smoke pervades the spirit, washing away the accumulated grime of negative influences that may have adhered to it. Burning a joss-stick is a familiar use of incense: you may light one simply for its pleasing effect, but when the burning is performed with conscious intent the effect is magnified.

Native Americans use several herbs in purifying ceremonies, notably sage, sweetgrass and cedar, either separately or together.

wormwoods, which also favour dry conditions but are found more widely. Sage has a transformative property, working upon negative energies that are somehow clouding an aura. It changes these negative influences to enable them to act for the benefit of the person, place or object whose aura is being cleansed.

CEDAR

A purifying incense, cedar is very beneficial for healing on both physical and spiritual levels. The small, flat leaves can be burned alone on a hot rock – as in a sweatlodge – or on a hot coal, or they can be mixed with loose sage into a ball for burning. The sharp, sweet smoke produced is very refreshing and calming, having an uplifting effect on the spirit and enhancing clarity of mind.

CEDAR CLEANSES THE SPIRIT AND CLEARS THE MIND.

SAGE

The term "sage" is a catch-all for the main herbs used in spiritual cleansing. Many varieties of sage and sage-like plants are used, including White Mountain sage, which grows mainly in California, and the sagebrushes and

WHITE SAGE TRANSFORMS NEGATIVE ENERGIES.

SWEETGRASS

Also called "Hair of the Mother", sweetgrass is a tough, fibrous plant that grows in wetland conditions. Often used to make braids, it attracts beneficial energies to the user, calling on spirits to give strength and guidance.

SWEETGRASS IS USUALLY BRAIDED BEFORE BURNING.

MAKING A SWEETGRASS BRAID

Making your own braid gives greater significance to its burning.

1 Tie one end of the bundle of sweetgrass, divide into three sections and braid.

2 Once the sweetgrass braid is lit, extinguish the flame so that the grass smoulders for a short while. Waft the braid in front of your face to inhale the smoke, and repeat four times.

INCENSE

There are many different incenses to choose, with different aromas and properties. Frankincense has been prized for thousands of years. It is a natural tree resin which is often used as a meditation aid. Piñon is a tree resin from North America with cleansing and clarifying properties. Temple Balls are a blend of gums, herbs and oils including elemi, juniper and sandalwood. They cleanse the air, affect atmospheres and relax the body.

INCENSE SMOKE AFFECTS SPIRITUAL AND PHYSICAL LEVELS.

FRANKINCENSE (GRANULES), PIÑON (RED NODULES) AND TEMPLE BALLS ARE JUST A FEW OF THE INCENSES THAT ARE AVAILABLE.

SMUDGING

When you are smudging you are cleansing the aura, the energy shell of a physical body. Just as your body can become dirty, so too can your aura, and smudging can clean it. The smoke from the herbs used acts like the soap when washing, picking up the negative grime that accumulates to the aura. Following the same analogy, the wind from a smudge fan acts like the water carrying away the grime as it blows through the aura, leaving the smudgee feeling refreshed and uplifted. Visualization, altars and smudging are all ways of creating a sacred space both within and without, and are powerful aids in aligning with the natural forces of the universe.

PERFORMING A SMUDGE

While smudging someone, focus on the cleansing action of the herbs and hold the intent of cleansing the recipient in your mind. Sense the person's energy as you work, and imagine the smoke carrying away the grubbiness as it blows through the aura. Stroking with the fan serves to preen the aura and signal the end of the ritual.

1 Light the smudge stick and use a smudge fan or feather to fan it until it is glowing strongly and there is plenty of smoke.

2 Your partner should stand with arms outspread, focusing on the cleansing. Fan the smoke over the body, starting at the head and finishing with the feet.

3 When you feel the ritual is complete, finish off by stroking down the aura with the fan, ending the strokes with a flick.

SMUDGE STICKS

Smudge sticks are densely packed bundles of herbs, often including mixtures of white sage, sweetgrass and cedar, which can be obtained from most alternative or New Age shops. When lit, they smoulder slowly and produce clouds of fragrant smoke. This smoke can be used for smudging, or just to scent a room with natural incense. When smudging, the smoke is wafted over the body using a smudge fan, or just a single feather.

SMUDGE STICKS MADE FROM CEDAR, SWEETGRASS AND SAGE.

SMUDGING A PLACE

You can perform a smudging on places and objects as well as on people. The smoke from smudging will help to cleanse or purify a small area of a room or an entire building, and can also be used on an item, perhaps before using it in a ceremony. When a new home is first moved into, smudging can help clear any residual influences of the previous occupants, especially if you can perform it when the place is empty. Whenever or wherever you feel it is appropriate, smudging can be performed.

The principle is the same as that for smudging a person: cover the whole area and try to feel if there are any particular areas that need a little extra attention. You can finish off by drawing a circle in the air with the fan to close the ritual and seal the cleansing.

SMUDGING CAN ALSO BE USED TO CLEANSE AN AREA OR PLACE.

RITUAL

He watched the lazy curl of smoke spiral upwards from the dying glow of the sweetgrass braid. Holding the pinch of tobacco loosely in his left hand he raised his arm aloft as he offered it to the sky and sent his thanks flying from his heart. Stooping, he pressed his hand to the ground and recognized the Mother with gratitude. In turn, the tobacco was proffered to the four directions as he thanked them for their teachings. Finally, on bended knees, he placed the offering on the small rock altar and sat back on his heels as a sense of serenity and belonging washed over him.

GREETING THE DAY OUTSIDE HAS PARTICULAR SIGNIFICANCE.

We are all creatures of habit, with certain ways of performing various tasks, from cleaning our homes and ourselves to preparing food. What differentiates habit from ritual is the intent of the action. Performing an act with conscious intent has the effect of increasing the efficiency of that act. This is because the intent carries to other levels of your being. If you take a shower with the intent in mind of cleansing your spirit as well as your physical body, the overall cleansing effect is greater. In the same way, rituals help strengthen our connection with the universe. Just as vibrations spread across a spider's web or ripples radiate across water, a simple ritual can have far-reaching effects on you and those with whom you relate.

MORNING RITUAL

Greeting the morning is a great way to start a new day. Work out your own simple ritual involving a few stretches followed by a moment of quiet or meditation to collect yourself for the day. If you can be outside for your morning ritual it will have greater significance. The set of yoga moves called "Salute to the Sun" requires little time or space and the movements invigorate the body at the same time as the ritual strengthens the spiritual bond you have with creation.

EATING AS RITUAL

Food preparation and eating are powerfully symbolic activities, and a good time to incorporate ritual with day-to-day practicality. When you are preparing food, do it with love and appreciation of what has been supplied by the bountiful Mother to give you nourishment.

It is better to eat natural foods in preference to processed ones, and organically produced food in preference to intensively farmed products. This is not only beneficial to your health but also from a spiritual point of view. Foods that have been raised without recourse to pesticides and inorganic fertilizers have more goodness and flavour and a closer connection with the Earth, therefore more of those attributes are entering your body. As you prepare food endow it with love and appreciation every step of the way, do the same when you eat it. While eating, the food nourishes the body and the ritual nourishes the spirit.

EAT NATURAL, UNPROCESSED FOODS AS OFTEN AS POSSIBLE.

THE BREATH OF LIFE

Deep-breathing exercises also help to awaken a sleep-fuddled mind and vitalize the body. Scoop up armfuls of energy as you breathe in. As you repeat this sequence, begin to visualize a flow of energy, so that you are both gathering it in and giving it out, returning it to its source. The fundamental characteristic of energy is movement and if it is blocked it becomes stagnant in much the same way that still water does. By giving out you are allowing room for more to come in: the more you give, the more you will receive.

1 Stand in a relaxed posture, knees slightly flexed and arms at your sides, hands cupped loosely in front of you. Slowly take three deep breaths to centre yourself.

2 On the fourth breath, as you inhale, circle your arms up, keeping them rounded. Now exhale, and let your arms sink slowly down with your hands, palms down, in front of you, to return to the initial position.

Making an Offering

When you make an offering you are exchanging energy, as well as giving thanks. Leave an offering on your altar with gratitude for the day and your life. Tobacco is often used for such a purpose as it is regarded as a sacred herb by Native Americans and is used in their ceremonies and rituals. Salt, which is regarded as sacred by Celts, is also used for offerings, and both tobacco and salt are easy to carry around. You can also leave a small coin as an offering, or natural items like a pretty shell or pebble, a single flower, or a few nuts or berries that you've gathered on a country walk. It doesn't really matter what you leave, as long as it is significant to you, and your intent is clear.

MAKING AN OFFERING INSIDE

Your indoor altar might be permanently set up in a corner of your home that you have set aside, or it may be a very simple collection of stones, candles and incense that you assemble when needed.

Use your altar for offerings at particular times of the day or when you feel it is right to do so. A good ritual for night-time is to give thanks for the day that has passed, and to ask for dreams in the coming night to be clear and that you may remember them. Make an offering on your altar last thing at night, using incense and candles, and voice your request aloud to reinforce the intent with which you perform the ritual.

AN OFFERING OF TOBACCO ON AN INDOOR ALTAR.

A STONE LEFT AS AN IMPROMPTU OFFERING ON A TREE.

LEAVING AN OFFERING OUTSIDE

When you are taking something from the natural world such as a special stone you've found, or are simply enjoying a country walk, show your gratitude by leaving something behind.

1 To make an offering, gently hold whatever you wish to give in your hand and present it up to the sky.

2 Lower your hand and present your offering to the Earth to show appreciation to the Mother.

3 Hold it out to each of the four directions, north, south, east and west, keeping in your mind the connection between all things.

4 As you leave the offering in your chosen place, voice your thanks and intention: "I offer this in gratitude for the gifts given, in honour of creation and my part in it."

SHAMANIC TOOLS

The shaman can use a number of objects, or tools, to assist in connecting with the spirit that weaves through creation. Because we are dealing with a natural force, the most desirable objects to use are gathered from the natural world. Feathers, stones, sticks and so on are all recognized as potent allies that a shaman can utilize to help them commune with other parts of creation. Other tools, however, are those which are hand-made for a specific purpose. The most recognizable and universal of these are the drum and rattle, used by shamans from many traditions to aid in journeying and achieving a trance. Other tools that are used in modern shamanism are the smudge fan and the godseye.

THE SHAMAN'S DRUM

The drum is a well-recognized symbol of shamanism, carrying deep primal undertones that reach into the atavistic recesses of the human soul. The heartbeat is the first sound a child hears in the darkness of the womb and the drumbeat evokes the link between mother and child. But it reaches further back and deeper in and, representative of the heartbeat of Mother Earth, it is full of vibrancy and energy.

The most desirable drum is one made by hand, using natural materials, because a well-made drum is a powerful tool, holding not only some of the energy of the materials used in its manufacture, but also some of the energy of the maker. Although it is possible to buy hand-made drums, a great deal

THE DRUM ASSISTS SHAMANS IN JOURNEYING, ITS BEAT OPENS GATEWAYS AND CARRIES THEM THROUGH TO OTHER WORLDS.

THE ENERGY IN TOOLS AND ARTEFACTS CAN BE UTILIZED BY A SHAMAN FOR VARIOUS PURPOSES.

of satisfaction can be derived from making one yourself. Drum-making workshops are held in a number of places.

Before using a drum for a ceremony, ritual or journey, make an offering to the spirit of the drum. The spirit is made up of the essence of the animal that gave its hide, the tree that gave its wood and the maker that gave their intent. The offering is given to honour the separate units that came together to make the whole. When journeying, a drum helps to focus the traveller in entering the spirit body and in connecting with the universal energy. Research indicates that the optimum drumbeat is around 200 beats per minute (bpm), so practise your drumming until this is your automatic rhythm.

NATURAL ITEMS CAN BE POTENT SHAMANIC TOOLS.

THE SHAMAN'S RATTLE

A rattle is a useful tool to signal intent to any spirit you may wish to call upon. Because of this it is a good way to open a ceremony or ritual, in addition to voicing your desire aloud. Of course it is also a good complement to any singing and chanting

PRACTISE YOUR DRUMMING TECHNIQUES.

that may occur. The rattle can also be used for healing purposes, to call in allies to aid with a problem or cure. A very simple rattle can be made by putting dried peas in a jar or tin but, as with the drum, you

A RATTLE OF SEED PODS.

can buy one, or you may be able to find a workshop where you can learn to make one from hide mounted on a wooden handle and filled with dried beans or pebbles.

TOOLS FROM NATURE

Everything has its own energy, and shamans can utilize this to synchronize their own energy with that of a tool. In this way a feather can assist a shaman to fly on a journey; a staff or wand cut from a certain tree can allow insights into the properties of that tree; a stone or crystal can give access to the strength and wisdom of the Earth.

SMUDGE FAN

A smudge fan is a very simple tool to make and is very pleasing to use. It can be elaborate or simple, consisting of feathers mounted on a handle or just bundled together and decorated with small beads and bells. Feathers make very good smudge fans and have the advantage of holding some of the energy of the birds that gave them. For example, eagles and associated birds of prey symbolize the ability to fly high and see far; owls, with their renowned night vision, represent the ability to see inside or beyond the veil of reality; ravens and crows have a long history of occult links; turkeys symbolize abundance. You can always find feathers while out walking, so pick them up and see if they convey any sense of their properties to you.

COSTUMES AND ARTEFACTS WERE ALSO IMPORTANT TOOLS, AS WITH THIS MONGOLIAN SHAMAN.

SMUDGE FANS CAN BE ELABORATE OR SIMPLE.

MAKING A GODSEYE

A godseye is a representation of the spiral of life and the universal connection of all things. It is a weaving of bright yarn around a framework of two crossed sticks and serves as a visual reminder of the unity of the universe as well as being pleasing to the eye and simple to make. The colours are bright to influence the subconscious mind. It can be as large as you wish to make it or you could tie several small ones together to make a network. It can be decorated with feathers and beads or left as it is. The choice is yours.

1 Tie two sticks of equal length together so that they form a cross. Starting in the top left quadrant and keeping the yarn taut but not stretched, start the weave by taking the yarn diagonally across the north-south stick down to the bottom right quadrant. Wind the yarn around the back of the north-south stick and bring it up to the top right quadrant.

2 Then wind the yarn around the back of the east-west stick and bring it over to the top left quadrant. Wind it around the back of the north-south stick and bring it down to the bottom left quadrant. Then wind the yarn around the back of the east-west stick, which brings you back to your starting point in the top left quadrant of the godseye.

3 Repeat the process and the godseye will expand. To change the colour, simply tie a new length of yarn to the one that you are working with. To finish off tie the last end around one of the arms of the cross.

DREAMWORLDS

To enter a dreamworld is to enter a place where anything can happen. It is a magical world of limitless possibilities, where the dreamer can fly, shapeshift, walk through solid objects or swim in the sun. And, especially while the dream is going on, it is every bit as real as this common reality that we all share in our day-to-day existence.

A dream is a way for the spirit self to communicate with the physical body, relaying information in allegorical frames that relate to the dreamer's life and experiences. Because the inner dreamworld reflects the outer world of the dreamer, it follows that a change in the outer world will result in a

THE DREAM OF JACOB BY FRANS FRANCKEN II.

KEEP A JOURNAL TO RECORD YOUR DREAMS.

change in the inner dreamworld. To go a step further, because all worlds are dreams, a change in the inner dreamworld will effect a change in this outer world. This idea that we all dream our own world into existence is not a new one, and if we are the creators of that reality we must, by extension, have the ability to change it by changing the dream. Dreaming is an important human activity and changing a dream is an empowering method of altering circumstances, behaviour and responses.

A shaman recognizes the validity of those other worlds and also accepts that this world, which we inhabit, is the dreamscape of some other reality. This is how strong, experienced shamans can perform

magical or superhuman feats; they can enter other worlds at will and project them to such an extent that they can be experienced by an observer.

Record your dreams in a journal both for future reference and because they can offer valuable insights into life situations. Keep a pad and pen by your bed so that you can write dreams down when they are fresh, because they tend to slip away from the wakening mind very easily.

To work with a dream with a view to changing or interpreting it, you need to return to it: that is, to recall the dream and play it through again in a relaxed and conscious state. Being relaxed allows your intuition to flow more freely and enables you to use your creativity to a greater degree. It is this interplay of intuitive creativity that allows you to gain insights from dreams and to effect a beneficial change in them from which you can move forward.

RETURNING TO A DREAM

To return to a dream use these simple steps to focus your mind and then release it.

1 Perform a small ritual beforehand: light candles to symbolically give you inner illumination to help guide you.

2 Make an offering and voice your intent. Why are you returning to the dream? For understanding? To change it?

3 Sit or lie comfortably where you will be undisturbed and relax yourself with deep diaphragmatic breathing. When you are relaxed, start the dream again and focus on what occurs.

WORKING WITH DREAMS

When you are back in your dream, politely question the characters and even the places involved: "Who are you? Why are you here? What are you telling me? Why am I here?" Go with the first answer that comes to mind but don't accept "No". A character may run away, or try to frighten you, don't be intimidated, follow them – they will lead you to an answer. If you want to change the dream, use any of the techniques discussed in the following sections and allow your creative intuition to flow.

More often than not, the main characters in a dream are manifestations of aspects of the dreamer. For example, disturbing dreams – perhaps involving death or violence of some kind – are not necessarily portents that some harm is about to befall the characters involved. Rather, the injured parties

DREAMING IS AN IMPORTANT ACTIVITY.

represent aspects of the dreamer that are being harmed, perhaps by not being allowed their full expression in the waking world, and that harm has a detrimental influence on the whole. By questioning the characters in the dream you can determine what aspects of your personality are trying to communicate with you, such as the child-self or the male/female-self.

A DREAM OF THE EAST BY JEAN-JULES ANTOINE LECOMTE

DREAM INTERPRETATION

The information that dreams are trying to convey can be divined by the simple expedient of questioning whoever or whatever is in the dream. If you can practise lucid dreaming (which means that

A DREAM OF LATMOS BY SIR JOSEPH NOEL PATON.

DREAM JOURNAL

Dedicate a special book or folder as your dream journal. Use it only for recording your dreams and keep it by the side of your bed. If you wake in the middle of the night quickly note down the memories of your dream, and in the morning make sure recording your dreams is the first thing you do. The details of dreams fade quickly and it is important that you retain as much of them as you can for working with and interpreting later.

you have volition in that dream and can control it) so much the better, because the questions can be posed there and then. If not, the questions can be asked in recollection.

To determine whether or not you can dream lucidly, all you do is try to perform a voluntary act in the dream. Attempt something simple, such as looking down at your hands or feet. Just work with it and see what can be done. If you wake with the memory of a dream, run through it to help fix it or, even better, write it down immediately. If possible, go back to it there and then, although it can be done at a later date; it is possible to return to dreams weeks or months after they occurred because that happens to be the appropriate time to return.

Changing dreams

The empowering ability to change your dreams has effects in this world, according to the shamanic premise that all worlds are in fact dreamscapes. Invariably, the dreams that we want to change are ones that cause fear, pain or anger, and by taking control over them in the dreamworld they manifest in, we are affirming our strength here, in this world.

When changing a dream don't try to force things to happen, just let your intuition flow and allow your creativity to come to the fore. Remember, anything can happen in a dream, so don't restrict yourself to the physical constraints of this world.

BELINDA'S DREAM BY HENRY FUSELI.

THE DREAM OF SIR LANCELOT
BY SIR EDWARD COLEY BURNE-JONES.

There are a number of ways in which you can change dreams. If the dreams are complete they can be altered by changing what occurs in them or by changing how you, the dreamer, reacts to what goes on. If the dream is incomplete it can be continued with creative intuition.

CHANGING WHAT OCCURS

Say you have a dream in which you feel powerless, perhaps chasing someone or something which eludes you. A way of changing that type of dream is actually to catch whatever it is that you are pursuing. They may continue to escape when you re-enter the dream but be persistent and persevere

until you reach your goal. This is a self-empowerment technique which returns the control to you. When you can confront whatever eludes you, it may lead to an altogether unexpected insight.

CHANGING YOUR RESPONSE

In a similar way to changing the dream, changing your response is a method of taking control. Fear dreams are often recurrent, and many feature being chased or stalked by some unseen or barely glimpsed presence. This can cause a great deal of anxiety and the dreamer may wake up short of breath and with a pounding heart. A way of taking control in this situation would be to transmute the reaction: instead of being tense and afraid in the dream, be lighthearted and happy. This will help dispel anxiety.

EXTENDING A DREAM

Most of us have experienced dreams that end prematurely when we wake, usually with a fearful start. A good way of changing this type of dream is to allow it to continue and see where it goes. Simply recall the dream and, at the point where you woke up, carry it on using your creative intuition. A typical situation in this type of dream is that the dreamer is falling, which can signify a leap into the unknown. The dream usually ends abruptly just before impact with the ground (thank goodness), but who knows what might happen if the dream was allowed to continue? Perhaps the ground might open up to allow safe passage, or maybe it would turn out to be soft and resilient. A good way to find out is to allow your creative intuition free rein and take that leap.

THE SLEEPING BEAUTY BY THOMAS RALPH SPENCE.

JOURNEYING

She became aware of subtle harmonics within the drum's pounding rhythm, a cadenza that meshed with her own internal beat. They sang just at the edge of her hearing and pulled, enticing her in deeper; a sweet siren-song that promised much if she would only surrender to the power of the drum. The throbbing thunder evoked a herd of wild horses galloping across a wide wind-swept plain and her spirit ran with them, riding the tempo as it opened a gateway to another realm ...

Unique to shamanism, the practice of journeying is a very powerful way to gain insights into problems, to look for healing, to seek allies or just to relax. When you journey, you enter a different world. It is essentially one that you create and guide yourself through, although your conscious self relinquishes control to your spirit. We have already explored the concept of sacred space and this is a good place to start a journey.

THE ROLE OF THE DRUM

A drum is useful in journeying and it is good to have someone drum for you, as a regular rhythm of around 200 beats per minute aids the focus needed for the opening of a gateway. It is good to build up the rhythm gradually to allow the traveller to become acclimatized to the adventure.

At first it is best to journey for a set time of around five minutes. At the end of this period the drummer can initiate the return with a call-back signal – say, four one-second beats followed by some very rapid drumming. With experience, the drummer will be able to use their intuition to tell when the journey is complete. Your power animal might be able to tell you when to start the call-back.

Making a drum tape for your journeys is very useful, as you can record several sessions of various lengths and incorporate your own call-back signal.

We all have the ability to journey to different worlds, and indeed do so when we dream. As in dreams, these otherworlds are places of limitless possibilities, where information is relayed in a format the journeyer can relate to. Unlike dreams, the journey to another world is undertaken with conscious intent and with a specific goal in mind.

PREPARING FOR A JOURNEY

When journeying to another realm, it is important to be open to whatever may happen and to anything you might meet. Trust your intuition, because what first comes to you is the right thing, whatever it may be. Just go with the flow and don't try to force anything. Remember that you have control over what you can accomplish in this otherworld that you travel to and don't be inhibited by fear. Be creative in circumventing problems and challenges that may arise.

As with physical travel in this world, if you prepare properly for a journey, things will go much more smoothly and it will be a much more relaxing and fruitful experience. A simple ritual helps to prepare you by centring you and focusing your attention on the journey you are about to undertake.

1 Gather your tools together and create a comfortable place where you feel relaxed and safe from disturbance. Light a candle for inner illumination and contemplate it quietly for a while.

2 Smudge yourself, the tools and your surroundings. Make an offering to the spirit of the drum and voice your intent: "I call on the spirit of the drum to assist me in this journey to meet my power animal/ find a power object/gain insight, and I make this offering in honour of you and in gratitude for your aid."

3 When you are ready, sit or lie comfortably and breathe deeply to get relaxed. Start the tape, and compose yourself as the drumming begins, maintaining deep, regular breaths as your journey commences.

Power animals

A power animal is your own personal spirit ally which takes the form of an animal. It is an ally that can accompany you on future journeys and give you guidance and wisdom.

Animals have always had great significance to native peoples all over the world and throughout history. In any culture, certain animals are thought to embody traits and strengths that are relevant to the history and geography of the culture.

Because there is such a diversity of creatures and cultures, a number of animals have come to represent the same characteristics. For example, the tribes of the north-west Pacific coast of America, living at the edge of the sea, revered the orca as a holder of great strength and wisdom, whereas to the plains tribes of North America, who had never seen a killer whale, that totem was fulfilled by the bison.

Whole books have been written on the symbolism of animals. This list represents a few of the more common ones and some of their counterparts from different cultures.

Nowadays, we are familiar with animals from all over the world and you may meet a power animal that has no general cultural significance, but the important thing is what that spirit represents to you. What strengths does it convey? What does it teach you?

EAGLE FLIES HIGH.

Eagle is associated with the ability to fly high and free, without fear and with the gift of far-sightedness. The eagle symbolizes the restless male energy and the quality of seeking and striving for higher goals. Similar totems include the buzzard and the condor.

Bear lives fully in the summer, retreating in the winter to hibernate and renew earth connection. The bear represents the receptive female energy, having the ability to go within to seek answers. A similar totem is the badger.

BEAR LOOKS WITHIN.

WOLF IS INDEPENDENT.

Wolf, fiercely loyal and true, still maintains its freedom and independence. A similar totem is the hound or dog.

Coyote, related to the wolf, exhibits the trust, innocence and playfulness of the child that is present in all of us. Coyote is also the trickster, and through mischief can expose pretensions and foolishness in others.

BISON IS THE WISE PROVIDER.

DOLPHIN IS AWARE AND UNDERSTANDING.

Bison evokes the strength and wisdom of the elders, providers for and protectors of the people. Similar totems include the bull, the reindeer and the orca.

Horse runs like the wind and is capable of covering distance with endurance. The horse symbolizes swiftness, freedom and faithfulness. A similar totem is the elk.

Dolphin represents understanding and awareness and is possessed of a gentle, loving energy. Similar totems are the manatee and the deer.

Owl hunts by night and is able to see in the dark, flying on swift silent wings. Symbolically it represents the ability to see that which is indistinct, to pierce the veil of reality and understand hidden truths.

JOURNEY TO MEET A POWER ANIMAL

Meeting a power animal is a useful journey to start with because the animal can accompany you on future adventures. This is usually the first journey people undertake. It is not a deep journey but it does expand your awareness, taking you to the edge of your sacred space, where it borders the realms of other spirits.

Once you have prepared for your journey, sit or lie comfortably and breathe deeply to relax. Enter your spirit body, go to your sacred space and orient yourself.

Begin walking. As you do so, a path will become apparent. Follow the path and go where it leads. It will take you to the boundary of your sacred space. Take your time to acclimatize yourself and observe your surroundings. Wait, because the ally will come to you.

Pay attention to the direction from which it approaches: north is in front of you, east to your right, south behind you and west to your left. Relate your ally's approach to the symbolism of the directions given in "Blessing the stones".

THE POWER ANIMAL WILL COME TO YOU.

PAY ATTENTION TO YOUR ENVIRONMENT AND WHAT DIRECTION YOUR ALLY COMES FROM.

... The eagle swooped down from in front and landed at the edge of the cliff, regarding me with one bright, fierce eye. Turning away, it launched itself and I knew I had to follow. I ran for the lip and leapt into the void. My arms flattened and became wings and I could feel my shoulders working as I beat upwards into the blue vault higher and higher until we could see the curve of the horizon.

The animal could be anything and it may not be what you were expecting, but when it arrives, greet it warmly, touch it and give it love. Be aware of what it feels like and feel the love it has for you. Remember, the greater the detail the more real it will seem. If it feels appropriate, transform yourself into the same animal and run, fly or swim. Above all, have some fun.

When you hear the call-back signal it is time to leave. Thank the animal for coming and tell it you look forward to future meetings. Retrace your steps and return to the familiar area of your sacred space before leaving it and coming back to awareness of this world.

When you have returned, go over the journey in your mind or, better still, write it down to help fix the details. This will aid you in future travels and make it easier to access the next time you visit.

COYOTE REPRESENTS THE INNOCENCE OF CHILDHOOD BUT IS ALSO THE TRICKSTER.

FOLLOW THE PATH TO THE BOUNDARIES OF YOUR SACRED SPACE.

JOURNEYING TO OTHERWORLDS

Deeper journeys to otherworlds require going beyond your sacred space. The otherworlds that shamans journey to are many and varied and can encompass any number of features, because each is a construct of the shaman that enters it. Essentially though, otherworlds are confined to two realms and when you journey from your sacred space you can travel downwards to the underworld or upwards to the upperworld.

THE UNDERWORLD

Most shamanic journeys involve going to the underworld, which is not comparable with the hell of Christianity and other faiths, but represents the inner recesses of the traveller. It is not a sinister place but it is a place of challenges and adventure. A shaman enters the underworld to seek solutions and understanding. The challenges you might encounter are all manifestations of your own fears and problems. By confronting them and finding solutions in the underworld you are facing them within yourself and allowing your spirit to communicate the solutions to your conscious self. Because you are journeying within yourself, you are seeking an entrance that will lead downwards and in. Remember, to gain entry, you can transform yourself to any size and shape required.

ENTRANCES TO THE UNDERWORLD

The opening could be anything:
- a cave or crevice in the side of a rockface;
- a recess or a knothole in a tree;
- an animal's burrow in a bank;
- a wormhole;
- a well;
- a doorway or gate;
- a waterfall or stream.

THE OPENING COULD BE ANY SIZE.

A WATERFALL OR STREAM MAY LEAD TO AN ENTRANCE.

ONCE YOU HAVE PASSED THROUGH THE OPENING, TAKE NOTE OF YOUR SURROUNDINGS AND BEGIN TO FOCUS ON DETAIL.

LOOK FOR A WAY UPWARDS.

ENTRANCES
TO THE
UPPERWORLD

The opening might be:
- a gap in the sky which can be reached by flying or leaping;
- a cave mouth high up a cliff that you need to scale;
- a tall tree to climb;
- a mountain that pierces a cloud;
- a flight of stairs;
- a ladder.

confronting fears that lie within yourself, the upperworld is more concerned with seeking assistance from others, by meeting other spirits on an equal basis and sharing knowledge with them.

This realm is very light and tranquil, with a feeling of limitless space that stretches away forever. Because it is related to the higher self, it is reached by going upwards. As with a journey to the underworld, it is good to have some structure to follow to help maintain your focus. Because going upwards relates to the soul, a good focus to have is to connect with your higher self. This part of your being is calm and all-knowing. It is dissociated from the emotions that have such a strong influence on the physical, and can therefore give counsel with a dispassionate objectivity that will cut to the heart of a problem.

At first it is an advantage to have some structure to a journey because it is easy to wander off course. A good goal to begin with is to go and meet another shaman, a wise person who will give you something. It could be knowledge, such as insight into a problem, or it could be an object. Accept it gratefully and give something in return. If the gift is an object take it back to your sacred space, and leave it in a safe place.

THE UPPERWORLD

Associated with the higher self or the soul, the upperworld is the place to go to for inspiration and communion with other spirits. Whereas the underworld is about

THE UPPERWORLD IS A PEACEFUL, TRANQUIL PLACE.

AN ACCOUNT OF A JOURNEY

We followed a path with trees on either side. They twined together overhead, growing thicker, until the tree-tunnel became a shaft sloping into the Earth, big enough to walk down. It was roughly oval and felt warm and dry. We emerged from a hole in a bank and looked around.

The bank extended to left and right and a forest of pine trees crowded thickly up against it. My ally walked forwards and I saw that he had found a path. I followed him and we snaked among the trees until we came to a small clearing. Suddenly, a giant face appeared, childlike but with curly blond hair and a beard, tilted to one side with curiosity. It looked through the trees as if through the bars of a cage and

HELP MAY COME FROM ANY QUARTER.

ONCE YOU HAVE FOUND THE OPENING, ENTER WITHOUT FEAR.

reached out a groping hand. I thought about running but stopped myself and waited to see what would happen. The hand scooped us up and popped us into the creature's open mouth.

We scooted down a long, dark tunnel and were ejected on to a wide, snowy plain, flanked on either side by mountains. It felt great to be running together through the snow. We reached the edge of a sheer cliff, so high that there were clouds below us. We stood looking out over an ocean and could see an island in the distance, small and green. How could we reach it?

A huge eagle swooped down and seized us. Its talons were sharp and powerful but they held us gently. Then the eagle was gone and we were gliding down on our own, heading for the island.

We landed in a marketplace, crowded with brightly clad people who paid us no attention. I thought one of them must be able to answer my question (the reason for the journey) and I began asking at random. Everyone ignored me and I began to feel frustrated and angry, until my ally grasped my arm in his teeth and pulled me towards a narrow alley. He let go and looked at me before turning and walking into the dim interior, beckoning me to follow him with a growl.

The brick walls of the alley became the rock walls of a canyon which led to a cave. An old man sat watching us from the entrance. He stood up as we reached him and I asked the question again. He made no reply but touched his index finger to his forehead and then to my forehead. He held up a small mirror to my face and I saw a blue mark where his finger had touched me.

I thanked him and we moved on into the cave. When we came out we were back in my sacred space. The wolf was no longer at my side and I looked over my shoulder to see him standing between two trees. I went back to say goodbye and he bared his teeth at me (a smile or a warning?) before turning and melting into the undergrowth.

This extract from a dream journal describes a journey, which shows (apart from what a good time you can have on a journey) that the question that was troubling the shaman's mind had assumed gigantic proportions and was literally swallowing him up. Also, the shaman had been bothering too many other people for an answer, when all he had to do was look inside. And the bared teeth at the end? That was just the wolf laughing.

NO OBSTACLE IS INSURMOUNTABLE; BE CREATIVE.

JOURNEY TO MEET A SHAMAN

THE MOUTH OF A CAVE CAN LEAD TO THE UNDERWORLD.

As with all journeys, begin by performing the preparation ritual to focus your intent. State your reasons for going and request the help you might need.

Relax with breathing, enter your spirit body and go to your sacred space. Call for, and greet, your power animal. Begin walking and, as you do, look for that opening that leads down and in, and enter the underworld. Once you have entered, be aware of your surroundings as you follow the path to the shaman.

If you are confronted by obstacles or opponents, find a way around them or through them and do not allow them to bar your passage. Be as creative as possible in getting past anything that may stand in your way. Remember, you have control over yourself and that your power animal can help you. When you meet the shaman, be respectful and loving. Whatever they give you is precious, whether it is an object or an answer to a question, and should be received by you with gratitude.

When it is time to return, retrace your steps, find the path and get back to your sacred space. Put any gifts you may have received somewhere safe and say goodbye to your ally. Leave your sacred space and come back to awareness of this world.

Record the events in a journal, because the information given may not be immediately apparent and you may wish to read through it again at a later date.

YOUR PATH MAY NOT BE CLEAR BUT KEEP FOLLOWING IT.

JOURNEY TO MEET YOUR HIGHER SELF

Follow the preparation ritual and state your intent for the journey. Relax by breathing deeply, enter your spirit body and go to your sacred space. Call for, and greet, your ally.

Begin walking, looking for the entrance to the upperworld, and enter. Once there, pause and take a moment to observe your surroundings. Your soul might be right there or you may have to go in search of it.

When you meet your higher self, greet it with love. It is wise beyond words and only wants what is best for the whole of you.

THE WAY TO THE UPPERWORLD MAY BE SMALL BUT ONCE THERE, IT IS LARGE AND AIRY.

Pose any questions you may have and receive the answers gratefully. They might not be what your physical body wants to hear but they will be honest.

When it is time to return, thank your higher self for the meeting and retrace your steps back to your sacred space. Say goodbye to your power animal and come back to awareness of this world.

Record the journey and any insights you may have been given to help clarify them and for future reference.

JOURNEYING FOR OTHERS

Sometimes a shaman may be required to journey to the upperworld or underworld on behalf of someone else, for purposes of healing or to seek the answer to a question. The principle is always the same: go with a specific aim in mind and be open to what befalls you on the way to your goal. The meaning of the tests and solutions might not be immediately apparent, but ideas will manifest themselves to the conscious mind and answers will come.

Journeying on behalf of another person is a mutually beneficial undertaking and can form a close bond between the people involved. Sometimes a person may be too deeply involved or traumatized to journey with clarity for themselves. Someone else, removed from the immediacy of the situation, can be more successful in the venture, being able to see with a more objective eye.

SPEND SOME TIME BEFORE YOU START, "TUNING-IN" TO THE PERSON YOU ARE JOURNEYING FOR.

SOUL RETRIEVAL JOURNEY

A journey to find part of a soul is a beautiful journey to undertake for someone else. As the name suggests, the purpose is to return a part of a person's soul or spirit to its rightful place. We are often careless with our souls, leaving a part of them with someone else or losing parts in difficult times of our lives. These lost pieces of our soul are of no use to anyone else and mean that we are less than complete – weakened in such a way that it can take a long time to recover. By restoring an errant piece of soul to where it belongs, the healing process is facilitated and the recipient becomes more resilient.

Because you are journeying for someone else, it is beneficial to develop an empathy with that person, so an extra step is incorporated into your preparation. Sit quietly for ten minutes holding hands and feeling each other's energy, then perform the preparation ritual. Relax with breathing, enter your spirit body and go to your sacred space. Call for, and greet, your ally. You are seeking another's soul so the journey will take you upwards. Begin walking and look for the entrance.

GRADUALLY BUILD THE DRUM RHYTHM UP TO 200 BPM.

LOST SOULS ARE LOCATED IN
THE UPPERWORLD.

Once in the upperworld, locate the main part of the soul and note the missing area. Is it raw like a cut or has it healed like a scar?

Begin your search for the soul-piece. It could be attached to someone else's soul, or it could be wandering alone. It might be lost and afraid or comfortable and happy where it is.

Once you have found it, talk to it. Find out what part of the soul it is and why it left or was given away. Tell it that it has a rightful place where it is needed. Be persuasive and do not leave without it. When it agrees to accompany you, guide it back to where it belongs and see it settled back in and comfortable before you leave.

Retrace your steps to your sacred space, say goodbye to your ally and come back to awareness of this world. Relate the events in detail to the person you journeyed for and, if they agree, record the experience in your journal.

THE SOUL-PIECE COULD
BE ANYWHERE.

YOU MAY HAVE TO SEARCH FAR, BUT DON'T BE DISCOURAGED.

JOURNEY TO FIND A POWER OBJECT

While you are making a journey, you may receive a power object, something that is for healing, inspiration or empowerment. The object itself, once found, should be brought back to your sacred space and left there, but the spirit or energy of it is brought back to this common reality and kept with you. Of course, when you obtain the power object, you should remember to leave something in exchange, because that strengthens the link. An offering in this case works the other way around: you leave the physical offering in this world, and you take the spirit of it with you into your sacred space when you make a journey. This can be incorporated into your preparation ritual as an extra step. To find a power object perform the now familiar ritual of preparation, then make an offering

to signify the grateful receipt of the object you seek, taking the spirit of the offering with you. Relax with breathing, enter your spirit body and go to your sacred space. Call for, and greet, your ally.

Power objects are found in the underworld, so look for the opening and enter. In the underworld, look for a path or let your ally guide you to the object you seek. Do not allow obstacles or opponents to hinder you on your quest. Be adaptable in circumventing problems and keep an open mind. When you find the object, receive it gratefully and leave the spirit offering.

Retrace your path back to your sacred space and put the power object in a safe place. Thank your ally and say goodbye, then return to this world. When you have

A POWER OBJECT CAN BE NATURAL OR MAN-MADE OR A COMBINATION OF THE TWO. ANTICLOCKWISE: RIVER WASHED STONE, EAGLE FEATHER, FLINT ARROWHEAD, DEER ANTLER, BEAR CLAW PENDANT.

LEAVE THE OBJECT IN A SAFE PLACE, SUCH AS A TREE'S KNOTHOLE.

THE PATH WILL LEAD TO WHAT YOU SEEK.

received a power object on a journey, be aware of things that may come to you here, objects which may be a physical representation of the power object that you left in your sacred space. These things may not look like the article that was given to you, but they will have a similar feel, or energy, about them. They are often gifts from other people, but they could be things you see when you are out walking, or even shopping. The key is to be aware.

RECEIVING A SYMBOL

Symbols are potent images, and it probably won't surprise you to learn that, as a shaman, you can discover or create your own symbols for personal empowerment. Returning to the idea that dreamworlds and reality are essentially the same, symbols that appear in dreams and journeys have their own reality and strength. In essence, a power animal is a symbol, as is a power object, and just as you journeyed to find an ally or an object, similar journeys can be undertaken to discover a particular symbol to aid you in healing or self-empowerment. Such a symbol could take any form: a word, a picture, a song, a design or even a person. The important thing is that it is significant to you and that it conveys a strength that you can call upon.

Any symbol that you receive on a journey or in a dream can be represented physically in this world. For example, a design or an image can be drawn; a word or phrase can be written down. These images can be displayed around your home so that you can focus your attention on them to gain the benefits they offer. A song can be sung whenever necessary for the same purpose, and a person can be represented by a drawing or even a photograph.

THE SYMBOL YOU FIND ON A JOURNEY MIGHT BE INSPIRED BY AN ANCIENT SYMBOL YOU HAVE SEEN IN THIS WORLD.

You don't need to go on a journey to create a symbol but you do need to be in a relaxed state to let your creative intuition flow freely and to contact your higher self. Whatever forms your symbols take, you need to focus your attention on them to get the maximum benefits. It is not enough just to have them lying around. If the symbol is an image, spend some time each day concentrating on it; if it is a word, phrase or song, say it aloud or read it, and if it's solid, handle it and note its detail.

JOURNEY TO FIND A SYMBOL

Symbols are a form of positive visualization, so you need to focus on an area of your life where you would like to see some improvement, such as a new job or a different lifestyle. Once you have the concept in mind, perform a simple ritual to help focus your attention. Once you start receiving images or words, write them down or draw them as they come. Don't worry about fine details at this stage, because the main thing you are after is the form, and you can embellish it later. When you have finished, thank your higher self for helping you and see what you have come up with. There is no limit to the number of symbols that you can acquire or create, although if you have too many you may become a bit confused about what you are trying to achieve. As with a power object, be aware of things that come to you that may have a similar feel to them, things that may represent your symbol in this world.

1 Light a candle for inner illumination. Make yourself comfortable as you sit and contemplate the flame for a while.

2 Smudge yourself to cleanse and calm you. Smudge the tools you are using and the place where you will be sitting.

3 Holding a pad and pencil, close your eyes and breathe deeply to relax. Keep breathing deeply and concentrate on your objective. Ask your higher self to give you a symbol that will help you to achieve your aim.

CODA

The sáman, *weary after his long hours of dancing and chanting, turned to make his way down from the low rise where the ritual had been performed, back to the village.*

Pulling on his soft reindeer-hide parka against the encroaching cold, his senses were still buzzing with the resonance of the celestial symphony that played on and on, an endless stream of seemingly disparate airs that blended and melded to form the wildly beautiful melody of creation.

Rising and falling, the harmony trickled through his body; a delicate glissando from the sighing wind played counterpoint to the constant susurration of the trees. A high descant on the air was an eagle soaring amongst the strains rising from the land; the subtle thrum of water flowing beneath the river-ice, the heady rush of a hunter closing on its prey and all the others that joined to form the whole.

And there, a steady rhythm underlying the rhapsodic fugue, the great bass notes from the rocks of the Earth.

He paused in his slow progression as a new sound reached him. It was alien yet hauntingly familiar, like the distorted echo of his own song. He smiled secretly, knowingly as he moved on, certain in the cycles of life that turned and turned and turned ...

... The drumbeat faded in a buzzing harmonic as she came back to awareness, her body tingling like a plucked wire. She could almost still feel the intense cold, the chill of the landscape that she had travelled through; the snowy plain that had opened like a yawn beneath the pastel-streaked sky, a sky that had split asunder with the crescendo of the sunrise. It had all seemed so real, so solid.

And the old man that she had seen, alone in that wintry land with his secret, knowing smile on his painted face. She knew he had somehow seen her or sensed her as she passed.

Part of her was still there and, as she recalled his face, a circle wheeled across her mind's eye, turning and turning and turning ...

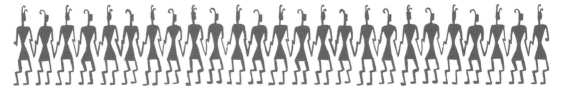

Useful Addresses

UK
Middle Piccadilly
Natural Healing Centre
for drum-making and
shamanic workshops
Holwell
Sherborne
Dorset DT9 5LW
Tel: 01963 23468

The Sacred Trust
for mail order items (tapes,
books, tools etc) and
workshops
PO Box 603
Bath BA1 2ZU
Tel: 01225 852615
Fax: 01225 858961

Arcania
for tapes, books, tools, herbs,
incense, etc
17 Union Passage
Bath BA1 1RE
Tel: 01225 335233

Lotus Emporium
for mail order incense, herbs,
smudge sticks, candles etc
Tel: 01225 448011

AUSTRALIA
Tranceformations
for shamanism supplies and
information
92 Dent Street
Ashburton VIC 3147
Tel: 613 9885 8783
Fax: 613 9885 5760
Web site:
www.tranceformations.com.au
email:
info@tranceformations.com.au

Nature's Energy
for crystals, meditation
tapes, incense etc
105 Glebe Point Road
Glebe NSW 2037
Tel: 612 9660 8342
Fax: 612 9660 5584
Web Site:
www.naturesenergy.com

Adyar Bookshop
for books, crystals, oils etc
230 Clarence Street
Sydney NSW 2000
Tel: 612 9267 8509
Fax: 612 9267 4719
Web site: www.adyar.com

US
Dance of the Deer
Foundation centre for
shamanic studies
PO Box 699
Soquel, CA 95073
Tel: 831 475 9560
Web site:
www.shamanism.com

Institute for Shamanic
Synthesis
4740 East Sunrise Drive
PO Box 336
Tucson AZ 85718
Tel: 570 529 1793

Flight of the Hawk Center
for Contemporary
Shamanism
PO Box 3157
Half Moon Bay, CA 94019

Tel: 650 562 1074
Fax: 650 726 7868

The Sacred Grove
for incense, candles, herbs,
books, tapes etc
1236 Los Osos Valley Road
Los Osos, CA 93402
email: sacgrove@silcom.com

The Four Winds Society
PO Box 2465
Palm Beach, FL 33480
Tel: 561 832 9702
Web site:
www.thefourwinds.com

Acknowledgements

The publishers would like to thank the following picture libraries
and photographers for the use of their pictures.

AKG London: 4l; 23tl; 10bl, tr; 11; 22br; 23tl; 42tr. Ancient Art
and Architecture: 22bl; 23br; 24; 26tl; 60. BBC Natural History
Unit: 50bl; 52bl; 54tl; 55t. E. T. Archive: 8tl, br; 9; 36bl; 38tr.
Fine Art Photographic Library: 40bl; 41tr; 42bl; 43. Images
Colour Library: 1; 17l; 34bl; 46t; 47bl, tr; 49bl; 50tr, br; 52tr; 55b;
57bl. Tony Stone Images: 12b, tr; 13; 14bl; 17 tr; 20b; 46b; 47tl;
48bl, br; 49r; 51bl, br; 53; 54r; 57tl, r.
Wildlife Matters: 15bl.

INDEX